Manifestations of Thought

Molana Shah Maghsoud Sadegh Angha,
"Pir Oveyssi"

 M.T.O. Shahmaghsoudi® Publications 

 M.T.O. Shahmaghsoudi® Publications 

Angha, Molana Shah Maghsoud Sadegh

Manifestations of Thought

Library of Congress Catalog Card Number: 97-069690
ISBN: 0-910735-70-0

Printed in the U.S.A.

Published by M.T.O. Shahmaghsoudi
Printing and Publication Center
10590 Magnolia Ave., Suite G
Riverside, CA 92505
U.S.A.

e-mail: angha_rs@pacbell.net

M.T.O. Shahmaghsoudi Headquarters
5225 Wisconsin Ave., N.W., Suite 502
Washington, D.C. 20015
U.S.A.

e-mail: mtos@cais.com
website: http://mto.shahmaghsoudi.org

Molana Shah Maghsoud Sadegh Angha

"Pir Oveyssi"

Contents

NOTE ON TRANSLATION AND TRANSLITERATION

In translating from the Persian, the masculine gender is used in references to God and human being (*"ensan"*). This is partly for convenience, but also because the Persian language has no distinct gender denominations; thus, the Persian pronoun *"ou"* may mean "he" as well as "she" with the proper meaning contextually determined.

Preface

Molana Shah Maghsoud Sadegh Angha, called Professor Angha by his students, was the 41st in a continuous succession of Masters (Pirs) of the Oveyssi School of Sufism, dating back to the time of the Holy Prophet of Islam in the seventh century. The Pirs of this School have presented the truth of knowledge in an unbroken chain of guidance for more than 1400 years. Born on February 4th, 1916, in Tehran, Professor Angha was trained from early childhood in the traditional gnostic and spiritual sciences by his father, Molana Mir Ghotbeddin Mohammad Angha, the 40th Pir, who was himself the son of Molana Jalaleddin Ali Mir Abolfazl Angha, the 39th Pir. The works of four great Spiritual Masters, these three plus Professor Angha's son, Molana Salaheddin Ali Nader Shah Angha, the 42nd Pir, have been the catalysts for the current Renaissance in Sufi art, music, literature and the sciences, and for making Sufism accessible to all who sincerely wish to learn.

Professor Angha was proficient in an amazing number of traditional and contemporary disciplines. He completed advanced studies in law, philosophy, literature, mathematics, physics, chemistry, nuclear physics, biochemistry, astronomy, and astrophysics. In addition, he was skilled in the traditional medicine of Iran, in the esoteric sciences of letters and numbers, and in Kymya or Iranian alchemy, which is completely different from what is presented as alchemy in the West.

This beloved and revered master attracted students from around the world. He passed away on November 17, 1980, in the United States. In his honor, his son has constructed, near Novato, California, a memorial building containing many fine examples of beautiful Islamic arts and crafts not known in the West. Those who visit comment on the atmosphere of harmony, peace and love which envelops those who enter.

This work, written 40 years ago, is a bridge between the traditional style of classical Sufism and the scientific orientation and language of the contemporary West. It is also a bridge between eastern and western conceptualization and religious orientation, based on the wisdom of inspiration experienced by a mystic of the highest and most profound level of cognition. Professor Angha gently, delicately and slowly strips away the veils to reality which characterize our thought and behavior, allowing us to attain a glimpse of the true reality beyond conventional boundaries.

Professor Angha is one of those rarities, the person who can transcend his own time, place and culture to not only perceive the universal essence of the individual human heart, but to live and write based on the revelation received through it. This book articulates the metaphysical, spiritual aspect of our being, and leads us to expand our vision beyond the constraints of this planet to the infinite dignity of the galactic realm, encouraging us to explore the vastness of our own metaphysical energy sources.

In eight succinct manifestos, Professor Angha summarizes the foundations of Sufi teaching, using illustrations primarily drawn from the world of science. If one were to follow his advice and heed the eight manifestos in every aspect of one's being, one would be able to attain the goal of Sufism, which is the development of the true Self, rather than the egotistical self. As the Prophet Muhammad (peace be upon him) stated:

"Whoever knows the true Self, knows the Creator."

The book is an invitation to expand the self, to develop the soul, to claim our inherent spiritual birthright. It is an illuminating lantern of hope for not only our personal future, but for the future of humanity itself.

Lynn Wilcox, Ph.D.

Introduction

If only the key to the one spiritual book
were discovered,
and the secret of the book of the
soul revealed,
we would need none of the words sealed
in silent books,
and yet would know the story whole.

هوالله العلی

"In God's Great Name"

I do not write this book to guide the reader, correct his thinking, or explain his current condition. My duty is simply to present the truth as I have discovered and recognized it throughout my lifetime. If someone were to ask me, "What is the reason for this presentation?" I would only answer: As sound waves are systematically emitted into space, sensitive recipients record that sound according to their capacity. The waves simply emanate from the source and are naturally received by the receivers who happen to be there, all in proportion to their capabilities. So it is with readers. The effects of any person's thought will surely reach and find, without the limitation of time, its suitable audience.

These pages reflect my discoveries of reality, as they stand in harmony with my inner essence. I am neither the wisest man of my time; nor is my word law. I try to present authentically from inner revelations, and take care not to deceive or distract the reader from the truth. We cannot be proud of memorizing the works of others, as they are not our own. That would be a kind of neglect that could prevent us from perceiving our own value and happiness.

It is quickly evident to everyone that any word, even the most fitting and logical word, can never fully convey its true meaning or the essence of the idea it represents. The word cannot transmit the meaning of the idea to the listener's ear and mind so that the listener envisions it as did the speaker. For example, if you would say the word "water" to a thirsty person, he would perceive none of the natural qualities and effects of water. Similarly, his hunger could not be satisfied by merely hearing the word "bread." With any word, we find this same deficiency.

There are additional problems as well. For example, sometimes the speaker is not fully aware of the significance of his own utterances. Even so, words themselves have no precise defined meaning, universally understood by everyone. When a speaker gives a speech, his audience perceives his words according to the experiences they have gathered. If they are not familiar with his words, they will never perceive his meaning. Indeed, each listener receives and interprets words according to his own unique experiences and circumstances. Each person has a very personal way of thinking, perceiving, and talking, so that the same words have different meanings and connotations for each listener. A true exchange between two people can thus only take place if a convergence of mind and experience occurs. It is on this delicate premise that developing understanding must take place.

Descartes[1] wrote that no one learns as much from another as from his own experience. Often, we experience intellectual discussions where it seems that the topic is understood and comprehended, only to later discover that the participants have each interpreted a different meaning for what was said.

Words are simply abstract symbolic representations of objects and qualities, which people use to communicate with one another. To expect to find deep meaning or creativity in words only exhausts the mind and imprisons the searching soul. Words alone cannot improve the mind or provide spiritual guidance or devotion. Leibniz[2] stated that, when the qualities of something for which we have only a verbal description lead to our understanding of it, we cannot be sure of accuracy. Descriptions may mislead us. Truths, by themselves, are not related to words.

My purpose is not to undermine society's agreements about the usage of words. My intent is to show that, although the truth may be present, it cannot be understood, heard, or illuminated through words alone. No one perceives meaning only through words; instead, we experience meaning through the depth of our being--the spirit. We understand perfectly only with the combined totality of our senses, emotions, mind, and spirit. It is then that we discover the true meaning of something. Everything exists in its own reality, and that reality's truth is not, in turn, further conveyed by the word that describes it. If we accept that purity of spirit is the basis and principle for conceiving meaning, then nothing is more valuable than studying the spirit, for knowing the spirit is the essential purpose of existence.

I suggest that, instead of spending time studying the silent books of libraries, we must search within our inner selves to find our own reality. We must study the book of the self, the innermost identity, and develop our brain's capacity to receive the sublime truth of the spiritual messages sent in waves by the clear and thoughtful minds of the teachers and mentors who preceded us. The truth cannot be captured in debates or by reasoning. Rather than analyzing the words of this text, I hope my readers will experience it in the depths of their existence, and then revise and expand it according to their experience.

My great Master, my father, guided and protected my mind with wisdom, patience, and spiritual mentorship. I offer what I learned from him without selfishness or ambition. With this gift, through my writing, work, and contemplation, if I am able to light a single candle of understanding, making a small step in the direction of benefit for the great human family, my life will not have been spent in vain. If not, I would fail to fulfill my mission, and my soul could not be content.

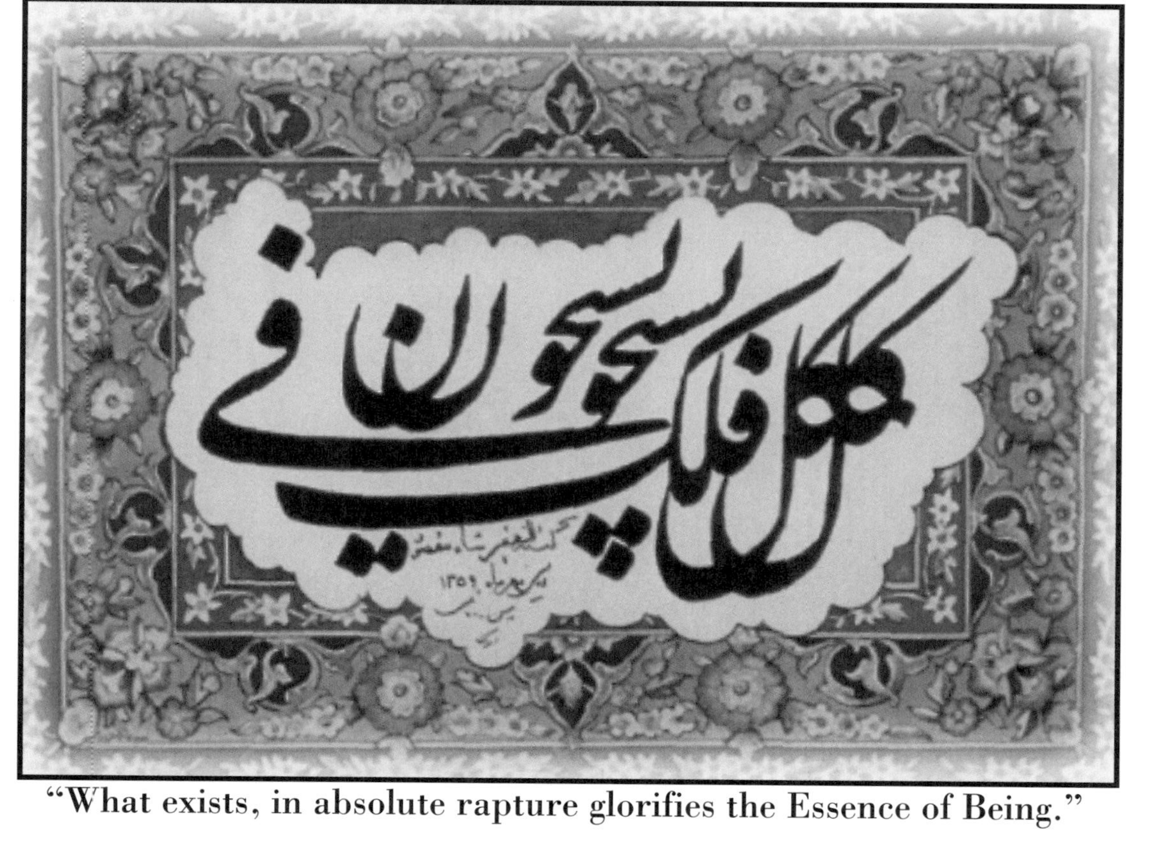

“What exists, in absolute rapture glorifies the Essence of Being.”

First Manifesto

Past scientific research is
a mere introduction
for the true scientist,
as true knowledge is based on
the consciousness
and essence of the human being.

If we considered the work of all the minds of today's scientists as the summit of knowledge, surely a final conclusion and certainty about the truth of nature would have been reached by now. A genuine scientist bases his thought within his own existence, and believes in a stable centrality within his own being. This centrality is the infinite essence of man. In this manner, the true scientist can perceive the 360 degree circumference surrounding his essence. He can also start from any hypothetical point surrounding this centrality to show the truth of existence through progressive computations. Although he can never get to the outer boundary of this essence, wherever he might be, he experiences the peace and tranquillity that originates in the truth of his essential nature and the nature of truth. He will, therefore, never be misled by comparing appearance with reality. The privilege of tranquillity and satisfaction emanating from within ensures that he does not present his hypothesis to the world as though it were an astounding event. He perceives his hypothesis as an introduction to knowledge.

When we envisage the ideas presented by astronomers and the considerable announcements made by observatories about other planets, it is possible to suggest that life on other planets may have made great scientific advances using electrodynamics and atomic energy. It seems that the stars and planets have diverse forms of energy: electromagnetic, atomic, solar radiation, and particle jets. When we view the alternation of light and darkness on the planets, we see a vast variety of patterns. There are clearly more possibilities than we know about currently. Perhaps other planets have made great scientific advances or even turned night into day using solar radiation and mirrors. Comparing the huge electrical force fields of Mars with our planet Earth is like comparing modern lighting with medieval lamps.

This example, and many others, help the beginning researcher to regard scientific theories, thoughts, and findings as an introduction to science. People who use rigid thought and who grow tired of investigating a subject cannot understand that the latest and newest method or scientific hypothesis is not the final truth. The discovery of a scientific theory is one of countless conceptual realizations that coincide with the potentiality of the scientist's mind in his ongoing search for perfection. Therefore it is not Newton's[3] or Galileo's[4] eyes conceiving actions and reactions, but their stable inner being which "sees" gravity and the rotation of the Earth. It is this stable inner centrality, in harmony with nature's process, that guides them to the infinite truth. Such scientists even try to extend their stable inner vision to superficial phenomena in order to research eternal reality. In contrast, the closed, insensitive person, whose centrality and essence have been forgotten, lost, and scattered in layers of natural reactions and appearances, is always surprised by stable perception and cannot stay focused on a constant truth. This person sees natural manifestations and scientific discoveries as unchangeable and static, so that in using them he simply reshuffles and repeats what was done before. Since the bases of inquiry and initiation are silent and dead within him, he has grown more compliant, imitative, and adaptive in his thoughts and actions. For example, he sees no possibilities or uses in a computer other than those it has now. This type of person, with his creativity dormant, merely imitates the efforts and accomplishments of others. He can never give an idea dignity or open himself to inquiry. He is, somewhat sadly, satisfied with whatever he sees in front of him.

Insensitive minds mistake introductions for essential truths. They behave like a child who has just learned the alphabet and repeats it loudly and enthusiastically to show everyone he has grasped something new. They may even think that no one has ever discerned this truth before. I recall a child who had just discovered a book on natural science, who asked me if I had ever read such a book or knew about natural science. He asked me in an arrogant way to let me know just how knowledgeable he was. But he never considered that his introductory book was just the beginning of study of this discipline. After his brief introductory reading, the child will, at least at first, treat his findings as an unchangeable and fixed law.

This static method of thought resembles an attorney defending his client in court. His defense must adhere to and be limited by the prevailing laws. In other words, his defense is constrained by the law and cannot go beyond it. The only thing he can do is explain the laws and present them as a defense.

The preliminary study of beginners is necessarily bound by past exploration, and when it presents additional investigation it refers to previous work. But if someday the beginner's mind matures and achieves greater capacity to perceive new and sudden clues, and if he is moved to ask himself the reason for his investigation into the past, his conscious mind may assure him that he has studied the past in order to understand the future. If the future is just another review of the past, however, his experience will remain naive and unscientific. Anyone who merely repeats a scientific or scholarly idea is not himself a scientist or scholar. Neither does the person who reads the Persian poetry of Hafez[5] beautifully have the poet's spiritual gift.

It is not uncommon to see famous people memorizing the words or works of great men and presenting them to an audience with such pride as if they themselves, by their recitation, had done something important. They have not yet noticed that they have done nothing to be proud of. Stagnant water in a sink will never be more wholesome than fresh running water. The wealth of one's memory, even if the details are recited, is no more valuable than a library. In contrast, a researcher genuinely inquiring into the work of those who preceded him can discover vital connections which can be used in his present and future explorations. Scientists have called this vital life force inspiration, or revelation.

I have described inspiration as a simultaneous recognition of the innermost personality and its perception of all things. It is a true and vital perception, a deep cognizance of the true connection between the scientist and the universe. We should treat revelation, which is a deep and true recognition within essential existence, as a high level of inspiration and insight. A theory born out of inspiration has not been intentionally created in order to confirm or deny previous thoughts. It stands on its own, in every detail, independent in its nature. Such a theory is only related to previous thought in a general way. For example, if a theory confirmed some findings and refuted others, it would not be seen as a scientific comparison, because the new theory was not developed with the intention of confirming or denying previous work.

It is Bergson's[6] opinion that a writer's masterpiece or an actor's performance of a scene will never give the audience true knowledge about the character in the story. The audience will not receive or recognize the reality and actuality of the character simply by reading the book or seeing the play. The absence of the characters' actual circumstances as well as the different interpretations in the minds of the writer and the actor, can lead to a misleading understanding of the character. This lack of identical experience proves Bergson's point. It is obvious that some things are relatively true and acceptable and some things are not. Since differences of thought are certain, knowledge, whether applied to the physics of nature or to metaphysical study, must be beyond sensory considerations and relative comparisons. Our sensory perceptions are always comparative and interpretive. They will not lead to creative discovery. It also must be noted that sensory perceptions always lead to comparison and interpretation because they are not new or original. Although one may have full sensory capacity, this does not mean one has full knowledge of anything. Seeing the character of the story does not equate to knowing or understanding that character.

If a play called Socrates[7], written by Plato[8], were brought to the stage and performed for an audience, the real Socrates would remain unknown. The Socrates in the play is just made up. Even in a great performance, what we get to know is the actor's interpretation, not the Greek philosopher. The real being of Socrates and the real details of his life cannot be accurately brought to the stage. Socrates, who speaks truth and acts on his truth, is not the same individual described by Plato or performed on the stage. The character of Socrates was as it was; and when Plato tried to introduce and describe Socrates, he was actually describing himself.

Genuine researchers consider those principles that are perceived in nature and proved by the intellect to be true knowledge and therefore original. Observations that are based on sensory comparisons are not stable truths and possess no spirit or essence. Such observations utilize the imagination and should not be confused with real knowledge.

In *The Great Secret*, Maurice Maeterlinck[9] described his sensory observation of a family who was gathering and carrying crops in the distance. At the same time that this picture with its appreciable use of color is glowing in the viewer's eyes, it is evoking joyous, sad, difficult, or painful memories. Its reality appears through the viewer's sensory experience and memories, but the qualities of the surface itself are unseen.

This careful discussion, which has some important psychological ramifications, shows us that sensory observations are conducted and regulated according to the observer's momentary mood and state of mind. This knowledge is based on sensory appearances and the framework in which they are received by the observer, not on the reality of the scenery and objects. For example, a view of a beautiful garden, vibrant with color at a fixed moment in time, elicits different concerns and feelings in a person sentenced to death who has an hour to live than it does in a prisoner with a life sentence, a poet immersed in his emotions, or a child.

Sometimes the conceptual qualities people give to a specific event may be completely different and contradictory. Yet we know there is just one event, one sensory picture, imparting different impressions. Since human characteristics and mental receptivity interfere with sensory appearances of real consequences and indications, it is likely that it is impossible to conceive of objects as they truly are. Thus external, superficial, sensory observations, which the mind photographs and analyzes according to its present qualities, are imaginary and unreal, and cannot be called true knowledge. As previously discussed, true knowledge is free of comparisons, relativity, and redundance, and is conceived of as intrinsic to the essence of man. True knowledge is manifested in the metaphysical quest that emanates from within, and thus it is differentiated from sensory perception.

" O' GOD, GRANT ME THY BLESSING SUBLIME "

Second Manifesto

Existence - The Ultimate Mystery

In reality everything in existence
is dependent on and a reflection of
the supreme law of the boundless universe.
Every particle and wave of existence
is confined to the law of the universe;
it has no choice in the matter.
What humanity perceives as choices
are the imagined limitations of particles
in the boundless whole of existence.

The reflection of the sun's light rays here on Earth and throughout the universe can only be observed at their starting point and their destination. We see the sun and the objects upon which its light waves are reflected, but the light waves themselves cannot be seen. Invisible and undetected as electromagnetic waves, light is seen reflected only at night from the other planets and stars. Earth's daytime, viewed from another planet, must appear as a planet does to us at night, reflecting the sun.

Powerful gravitational waves control and program orbits between the planets and nothing is outside their gravitational pull. Yet when we look at the Milky Way on a clear night and see the glittering stars and planets, we cannot see the tremendous gravitational forces controlling their course. The enormous force fields of these electromagnetic waves control the universe carefully and precisely, from the orbits of huge planets to the arrangement of atoms within molecules. Although we are generally unaware of these invisible functions of the universe on a daily basis, it is true that altering the forces of even one tiny atom could unleash the incredible power of atomic energy, which can change the whole universe, destroying the existence of nature as we now know it.

Man's sensory perception and even his highly developed imagination cannot fully comprehend the perpetual dance of electromagnetic power. Yet it is rather difficult to believe that this ever-present power has no influence on one's life, thoughts, and entire being. I cannot accept that a creature who comes into being from nature's womb and has been cherished and nurtured by nature's developmental process is no longer subject to this influence. Man is the culmination of a long evolutionary voyage within the universe of nature, and it is unacceptable for him to disobey or neglect natural laws in order to establish dominance and control.

Nature is a capable master, and does not violate or neglect the continuous and successive stages of eternal destiny. Even unimaginable accidents and obstacles do not alter its course. Nature leads everything, guiding every being in a specific direction. The power and dignity that you and I possess stem only from nature itself. Ignorance of this fact leads man to believe he is independent and self-determined. Nature cannot give what it does not have; everything in nature follows natural laws in a precise, organized fashion. Man misunderstands his power and influence, and believes "free will" bestows on him authority over the universe.

Nature, as our wise teacher, gives us guidance if only we are open to it. Study, for example, the force of atmospheric pressure. Every inch of the Earth is subject to it and obedient to it, as well as every material form, including man. In 1631, Descartes introduced his idea of vacuum. Vincenzo Viviani[10] continued to research this phenomenon with glass tubes of mercury. Later, Evangelista Torricelli[11] measured atmospheric pressure on the Earth, calculating the weight of 1 square centimeter of mercury 76 centimeters high. It is clear that every point on Earth, and everything on it, is constantly subject to this pressure and, in fact, dependent upon it. This natural force is obviously measurable and necessary to mankind, yet most people live their entire lifetime without even considering it. From the moment of birth, humankind has to obey this natural constraint without even knowing it. Consider, for example, the moon. This tiny sphere follows the Earth in every action, and yet its influence on the Earth is tremendous. Its rotations and movements have a powerful impact on the oceans and seas. How then could humans not be influenced by the forces around them? Humans are finite beings, tiny in comparison to the infinite universe. How can they possess free will?

Man's dependence on and vulnerability to nature is self-evident. The reflections of orbital gravitations on capable and susceptible minds, though perhaps invisible, are no less powerful than their effects on the planets. Without doubt, our minds are as susceptible to these powerful natural waves and forces as are the stars and planets. Perhaps, if our sense of hearing were more acute and focused, we could follow the directions of the sublime and superior thoughts in the sky that Newton and Kepler[12] viewed, just as we can follow gravitational orbits. The echoes of the validity of their thoughts are stable and independent, existing consistently throughout time. If gravitational forces lead the planets in orbit, why is it so difficult to suppose that a universal mind leads the spiritual development of the Earth's inhabitants? A balance in the spiritual and physical systems leads the mind of man to recognize invisible truths. A coalition of the physical and metaphysical underlies all of nature's waves throughout the universe. Just as man must obey the natural influences of air pressure whether he realizes it or not, a universal interdependence and reciprocity exists everywhere.

When a sudden intellectual insight occurs, one of nature's secrets is revealed to a fertile mind that is in balance with its physical and spiritual systems. At the point of this harmonic balance, physical and metaphysical waves can enter and resonate within the mind. There is a convergence of one's observations of natural reality and one's own spirituality, and one thus discovers an essential principle. The intricate, delicate, and subtle realms of life are then observed and experienced. In understanding the deep correlations between existence and one's being, physically and spiritually, one discovers a scientific law. By experiencing the harmony and union of one's observation of nature, one's conscience, and one's consciousness, one recognizes the natural law in the depths of one's heart and bequeaths it to humanity. It is clear that recognizing the stability of physical or spiritual laws is related to this encounter with the person's true personality and existential being.

If a person's physical and sensory systems work in isolation from his spiritual being, they will perceive whatever is familiar to them. To comprehend infinite natural wonders, we need extrasensory abilities and strengths, beyond those we now have. The closer our systems come to the infinite, the more infinite they need to be. To comprehend any concept that has an observable natural effect, it is necessary to explore the subject, break down its limitations and boundaries, and notice how it is related, attached, and interacting within the infinite. Otherwise one cannot observe a clear truth. Such deep exploration is not possible through one's sensory system in isolation.

In *Extra Sensory Perception*, Joseph Cenil writes that true knowing is the ability to conceptualize the electromagnetic waves that come to us from the objects around us. These waves pass through all materials and objects and are everywhere. He states that a clear-sighted man is one who can control his brain, so he can perceive the waves. Like a radio, he is able to tune out the static and receive the wave's signal. Newton's law of gravity, which states that the force of the gravitational attraction between two bodies is proportional to the mass of the two bodies divided by the square of their distance, is only the barest introduction to the field of waves in existence. Even animal magnetism is a study in wave relationships, though it is a study to be examined later.

When Cenil says that a clear-sighted man must have control of his brain in order to receive magnetic waves, he probably refers to a coordination between and harmony of the person's and the universe's physical and spiritual powers. This expands the brain's capacity of receiving electromagnetic waves. Although precise scientific and spiritual laws are based on observations and experiments that are practiced in the mind, we must also recognize the intelligence of the universe that triggered the quest for discovery in the first place.

It is clear that essential, fundamental conditions are necessary for the existence of and relationship between both transmitter and receiver systems. For example, if certain sound waves are broadcast on a special wave length, they are receivable waves. Yet these sound waves go unnoticed to an insensitive or deaf ear, even though they are broadcast throughout space. The same is true throughout life. Vibrant life surrounds us, full of physical and metaphysical happenings, but our knowledge is not equipped to understand the mystery and meaning of Existence. In order to perceive and understand the meaning of a concept, the first step is to realize that the concept and the conceiver must be on the same level and in harmony with all existent conditions. For example, we cannot conceive of sound or light waves in frequencies above or below our ability to hear and see. What we perceive is related only to our present abilities, and thus the results are merely comparative and relational.

Clear-sighted, thoughtful, intuitive scientists of the East believe that if all of a person's powers—mental and physical—are focused on a precise, delicate metaphysical point, that person can comprehend truth and reality beyond the sphere of habit and sensory limitations. This is precisely because the synergy of all of a human's strengths combined far surpasses the power of those strengths individually. When one reaches this concentration, the power of organized existence is in tune with the will of the intellect, and thus one is able to receive, recognize, and comprehend the forms of energy, subtle and sublime, throughout the universe. At this level of awareness, one is able to see and understand his spirit and divinity, and the energy and essence of his heart and soul.

Truth can only be known when a person can transcend outward appearances to grasp the meaning within, because real intuition and cognition means he sees things as they are. When the mind, senses, and spirit strive in harmony to know the conditions and circumstances of existence, there is a superior result. This concentrated striving is spiritual, and, throughout time, there has always been the gift of extraordinary individuals, as emissaries of God, who present themselves as a model and guide to encourage humankind.

The opposite of such synergy is fragmentation and the scattering of one's energy, which prevents true understanding. This kind of person is like a dismantled machine with no coordination between its parts; the machine, if you will, cannot do its job. Such people cannot act in their own best interests or develop fully. Their deeds are shallow and lack truth.

Third Manifesto

A noble society has a responsibility
to promote the sciences
and other fields of study,
and to encourage research by all those
with a yearning for knowledge.

When electromagnetic waves, infinite and universal as they are, intersect the magnetic waves of the brain cells of a sensitive and thoughtful mind, the interaction between the two leads to discovery and understanding. The secrets of nature, the seeds of new vistas for future civilizations, are opened to be explored by the willing mind. Certainly, publication and international recognition will result, if this mind is truly receptive and capable of expression.

We should be aware that if these introductory foundations of discovery are not encouraged and facilitated by the necessary means, their relevance will be postponed to a later time. There have been many excellent ideas and insights that have remained buried and obscure, having never seen the light of day. Like the sun hidden behind a blanket of clouds, or fire smoldering under a cover of ashes, these discoveries are hidden in dark corners of society, waiting to be expressed. Known only to the discoverer's mind and deprived of expression, such ideas are forgotten and absorbed in the infinite ways of infinity itself, ascending into eternity until the time for their reemergence arrives.

The famous German mathematician, Charles Friedrich Gauss[13], who dazzled the world with his brilliant mathematical concepts, might never have been known or recognized without the ongoing patronage of the Duke of Brunswick. Even his incredible brain cells could not have discovered and expressed his one hundred forty-six mathematical facts without practical assistance. Similarly, Augustin Cuchi's work and contributions were promoted by King Louis XVIII; if they had not, they might have gone forever undiscovered.

In order for scientific and cultural advancement to take place, suitable conditions and essential levels of support must be provided.

When we look at history, the highly developed countries are always at the forefront with scientific discoveries. Yet we cannot assume that the less developed countries have no great scientists or thinkers. They simply have a lack of support, and a scarcity of publications and means to value their discoveries.

Always, in every society, there are more charlatans than true scholars. The self-centered are always more numerous than those who genuinely seek to benefit humankind through science, the arts, and scholarship. When this small minority attempts to present its findings to the public, it faces the wrath of superstition and prejudice, of all those who feel threatened. With this type of response, scholars will never be able to express themselves and discuss their discoveries. Often, discoveries and ideas remain idle, buried in books and libraries, unappreciated and unused. Many great thinkers and scientists were ignored or ridiculed, their works overlooked until after their deaths. If there had been someone genuine in his wish to openly present these discoveries, he would undoubtedly have been falsely accused and wrongly prosecuted, as were Socrates and Galileo.

There are many who criticize scientists and thinkers for not publicizing their discoveries to the general public, in spite of the unreceptive atmosphere they may face. Yet history has shown us, time and time again, that the public tends to judge by its own limited thoughts and ideas, destructively ridiculing those who present new findings. Moreover, it is awkward to think of a scientist as a salesman trying to sell his goods, especially under very unfavorable conditions and despite society's widespread envy.

Many scientists have faced social disgrace and rancor, endured the hurt of empty gestures, and nevertheless continued their work and research. Consider, for example, Dr. Mesmer[14], who developed the theory of hypnosis. He was forced to leave his home, and live in the small village of Meersburg, Switzerland, where he earned his living as a physician. Still, in his free time, he continued his work and research on hypnosis while remaining unknown to those around him for his genius and accomplishment. His inner sadness is evident in his reply to an eventual invitation which he received after years of exile from the Berlin Academy. Dr. Mesmer wrote: "The sun of my life has traveled across the sky and is lowering to its horizon. My only wish is to dedicate my life exclusively to the specific scientific research in which I continue to discover practical uses and advantages."

Nowhere in the history of humanity is there a true scientist or thinker who enters his field for the purpose of fame or riches. Instead, scientists continue their research whether or not it is financially profitable. The selfish reasoning and self-praise of certain segments of society do not lead to the advancement of culture or knowledge. Social movements toward greater development for humankind, knowledge and spirituality, would strengthen and sparkle with beauty if it were not for the greed of the masses and those who mislead them. Unfortunately, the wise must always bear the burden of the ignorant, and this is the greatest injustice of all. Sadly, society does not care to encourage and support the gentle and sensitive minds and souls of its thinkers and discoverers.

There are many examples of this sad social situation. Galois[15], the great mathematician who invented Group Theory, suffered a life of disastrous misery and hardship. Yet in spite of hardship, and because of his respect for his knowledge, as he was dying, he wrote a two page summary of his work. Though suffering, he contributed to the book of human life so humanity would not be deprived of his knowledge. Like the candle burning by his deathbed that flickered out before the dawn, his sad death could not awaken the soul of an ignorant and prejudiced society.

The character of a nation depends on the scientific creativity demonstrated by its people. Science is not exclusively related to the repetition and explanation of the framework of past and present ideas. Past research, no matter how deep and thorough it may have been, is an introduction for the purpose of opening new paths and channels of life. Searching and discovering the hidden secrets of life formulates the developmental guidelines for social programs and the science of the future. Undeniably, there is enormous human talent and potential all over the world. Yet one can justly say that, in impoverished and underdeveloped nations, the doors of the university are closed to thinkers, scientists, and researchers with creative minds, as well as those with the industrial interests and skills to utilize mechanical and physical theories.

A university that does not accept, encourage, and transmit new ideas, discoveries, and positive solutions is merely a public library in which people review the ideas of the past. If we imagine that the purpose of science is to turn the economic wheels of society, the value of the production of a truly scientific institution managed by expert and determined scientists is still clear. Even in the most preliminary stages, true scientific research is not worth less than the results of mining excavation or agricultural development. The economic wheels of a nation must work in harmony with the energy and activity of its thinkers, researchers, and intellectuals. It is then that forward economic movement can occur. This important economic development and advancement benefits the living standards of all.

It is indisputably evident that individuals who lack the ability to think and who are unwilling to use their creativity productively are worthless in their disorder. Lacking the abilities to utilize their essential life energy, their centrality, they become parasitic, feeding off their society. In this situation, the university's role is to act as the brain for society, safeguarding its scientific and mental development and its practical capabilities. Otherwise, both university and society will degenerate, like a body without a mind that deteriorates as disease corrupts its ability to effectively manage its energy.

If a university functions like an interested institute, nurturing youthful, developing minds like a fetus nourished in the womb, its scientists will willingly offer everything they can. I have met many talented people in society who were eager to study and learn. Although I wished to help them, I have been unable to guide them alone.

If universities published the latest discoveries and findings and made these readily available to the public, they would not only benefit those whose works they publish, but they would also greatly enhance and educate society at large. This would encourage and reassure scientists everywhere. The transmission of scientific thought to the world is an essential primary step toward developing civilization.

Every human being aspires to noble accomplishments that will benefit humanity. If the spark of life shines in every society, striving for merely personal gain will eventually recede, and civilizations will attain the brilliance of which they are capable. Intelligent people can smooth the obstacles of life and pave the road of prosperity for themselves, their children, and future generations.

Fourth Manifesto

If our inner and outer character
is not changed,
our past will appear frightening
and prove to be shameful.

Physicists explain simple waves by dropping a pebble into water so we see the concentric circles that form around the point of entry of the pebble, and extend outward to the water's edge. The waves can best be described as transmissions through the water.

If one holds a tinted glass to look through at the sun, one would see large and small circles of refracted light extending outward from the sun. These are just like the waves that appear on the surface of the water. The waves are comprised of positive and negative oscillations of *sine* and *cosine* curves. These patterns of vibration exist at every level of nature. They are the general expression of natural structures that philosophers like Descartes labeled as indivisible units or atoms.

From the organization of the smallest particles—atoms, molecules, photons, electrons, etc. —to the most immense planets and vastest galaxies, the combination of waves and particles appears endlessly. Their movements and characteristics are patterned and relational. The endless, eternal, expanding and contracting waves of nature form particles, and the pattern of this combination is ever present throughout the universe, eternally and infinitely connected.

The constancy of this pairing of waves and particles throughout nature points to a fundamental unity, an inherent oneness of infinite existence throughout the universe. This does not mean that existence is purely physical; nor does it deny spiritual or metaphysical energies. The governing power of physical and metaphysical forces, the pure energies, in their ultimate aspects, lie outside of our sensory range of study, and lose their material forms and dimensions in the infinite. They are apparent to our senses, and occur naturally due to a series of interconnected events and proportionate relationships at a particular point in time. But, of course, they are not disconnected from the infinite.

Helmholtz[16] has predicted, "We will eventually get to the point where the essential study of physics will be to relate the appearances of nature to the vast, unchangeable, attracting and repelling energies of the universe." The interval or distance between these attracting and repelling energies determines the intensity and magnitude of their interaction. When these relationships are fully understood and these secrets of nature are truly known, this will, of course, be the supreme measure of scientific achievement. Once this tenet of Helmholtz is proved, we will be able to say that science has taken its first step toward discovering reality. From that point forward, proving the reality of existence will be experienced as more than mere verbal reasoning. In any case, the range of waves, as previously mentioned, have temporary forms that continuously and systematically act and react, transforming from one form to another.

If it were possible for a person to stand at a particular point in the wave of his own life, and have the vision to see this wave extending with its natural motion through his past and future, he would see all the states, qualities, and events of his life as the effects of the workings of his conscious and unconscious mind. Then he would be able to study his life, this vital and natural wave, as the reality of an unfinished book.

This description is a real possibility, as the human soul and essence is similar to what physicists call the fourth dimension, encompassing the dimensions of space and time. At the present moment, all the lower levels, stages, forms and limitations are visible and observable. To explain this, imagine, for example, that an ant is traveling from point A to point B in ten minutes. The ant itself is traveling according to the unit of its step, while an observer like us sees the whole distance in almost no time. The story of our body and soul is comparable to this example. Extrasensory perception, clairvoyance, dreams, and inspirations show us that the soul serves as an observer, unfettered by the body's dimensions of time and space. The body is the inferior stage of the soul; the soul is like a human and the body like his shadow.

The history of a person's life is like an infinite scroll on which all events and happenings are recorded. If we were to show this in detail, as if it were a motion picture, all the happenings of life would appear on the screen. Then we would see infinite existence and its ongoing construction unfolding in front of us. None of the mental and physical projections or events that would have been presented by this scroll are diminished or forgotten with the passage of time. The book of creation has imprinted it, stable and certain within itself throughout all time. Infinite existence is an absolute deed.

Thus the true events, incidents and adventures of our lives, which appear to occur naturally, are not futile, meaningless, or make-believe. Our present state is rooted in a constant and stable source that originates in the past and proceeds into the future. Any present outcome originated and was introduced in the past. If scientists were to present the theory that the present condition of every being includes its past history, no one would object that we have linked the present with the past. We cannot separate the origin of any human being from his present state and we must accept that his past is effective in the present as a continuous reflection of the infinite. Existence is like an unbroken thread, each individual event being unique yet in continuous connection with the infinite. We must explore the integral interrelationships and significance of things. If we look at the mechanical system of television, we see the camera transferring its wave images from one position to another, producing the picture of motion traveling from one point to another in the manner of an ascending and descending curve. It is this same reasoning, and the law of existence returning to the origin, that applies to this and all examples we can study.

We can, therefore, conclude that all beings, after going through their fated course of life, leave the imprint of their essence on the paths of life they have traveled. Their footprints can always be seen and reviewed in this continuous molding process called life. This predestined principle conducts the infinite universe with ultimate authority. At every point in this life journey, we inherit the realities and positions of the past. Action and reaction are the two impressions of the deed. For example, if a plant is not watered during the heat of late spring, the resulting yellow leaves will appear within two months. No matter what is done then to ameliorate the situation, the damage of the past will remain. I believe this idea will open up the field of medicine to look for the cause of illness in past history, so that it can be treated accurately and quickly.

Psychological research has shown that heredity and environmental training shape an individual, and that these factors have a direct influence on the person's present state of being. Likewise, it is evident that natural existence is traveling from an eternal point, unknown by the limited vision of man, to another unknown eternal point. In other words, this is the continuous journey of existence to itself, with no breaks, delays, or stops. Humankind is also marking its impressions and leaving its effects along this mysterious path. A person's deeds, thoughts, and imagination are acquiring form and shape, outwardly and inwardly, in infinite existence, as his body and soul are the center of his past interactions and the introduction to his future states. Humankind's physical and spiritual life in harmony with the passing of time is reflected in the face of existence. Our present state is an unfinished book, a projection on the screen of life. None of our past physical and mental states are eliminated or forgotten, because the book of creation has them stable and fixed within itself. Whenever suitable conditions arise they will manifest themselves. At that moment of truth, we will find that all the events of our lives are alive and real; they stand with all the conditions and consequences that surround them. At that point, our being will be an index or indicator of all that has happened before.

Every sound which goes out of our mouth carries its own attributes and remains in its own special wavelength. Its independence is preserved in existence from the origin of sound to anywhere in eternity. It exists in the line of its wavelength and a sensitive receiver can receive and transmit its precise pattern. The same phenomenon exists when we look at a film projected onto a screen. It seems as though the pictures only exist at the point of origin [the film] and the destination [the screen]. Yet it is clear that the pictures and their reflected qualities are also present in the space between the film and the screen. But changes in the shadows and lights, which appear differently in the film than on the screen, mislead us so that we do not recognize the sameness of these elements, wherever they are. On close examination we see that there are particles, atoms, molecules, waves, and metaphysical energies that make up all constructs of existence.

This eternal, destined presentation appears differently in different stages of existence. One is only able to see beyond appearance and perceive uninterrupted absolute reality through the harmony of one's senses and one's metaphysical capability.

Everything on every level of existence follows this natural law according to a predestined, prescribed order. This set program, seen throughout existence, is the equivalent of nature's free will. At this very moment, our system has recorded our entire past and its consequent qualities on a specific wave in time. Its imprint is there summarized in the wrinkled memory cells of the brain, and in our electromagnetic body. Because we are always trying to stabilize ourselves in the present, however, we do not see our existence as whole. Our future is unknown to us and we attempt to overlook our past.

True religious and ethical leaders, as well as learned men whose conscience is open to the truth, have always encouraged their followers to walk upon the path of worthy deeds, thoughts, and intentions. They warn the selfish of an eternal death. In spite of tremendous hardships, the lives of these great people are a pronouncement of this important invisible truth. The true character of these sages has merged with absolute reality; their thoughts and deeds are the law and essence of existence. They express the true and innate commandments of existence, carefully and precisely giving instructions to humanity. Following their instruction and teachings is like seeing through a powerful telescope that makes completely clear and understandable the true meaning of prosperity as well as that of adversity.

Fifth Manifesto

Particles are like numbers
appearing limited to us,
yet they are unlimited in infinity.
Nothing in the universe contradicts
its true wisdom and discipline.

If we look at the existing and hypothetical natural laws that we use to describe the process of nature, we discover that the cells of the human body are different from consciousness and understanding. A person's true essence, his consciousness and understanding, cannot be defined by the body. All the dualities we "see"--good and bad, unity and separation, eternal and ephemeral, light and darkness, motion and stillness, existence and non-existence--,all these and many others are projected by our limited perceptions as we form contrasts and make comparisons. Our sensory perception cannot show us true reality because our perceptual process is limited. Our senses use contrast and opposition, making limited and unreal observations, based on their own natural, necessary restrictions and circumstances. Scientists today are aware of the instability of the perceptual process and thus they seek to develop factors of reliability for their research. If we use the laws of Earth's magnetic or gravitational fields, we see these forces throughout millions of galaxies and stars, governing all living organisms and inhabitants. But if we tried to understand the mystery of existence using wave expansion or accumulation as a perceptual measure, our findings would be limited.

The mysteries of existence are only perceivable through infinity, where all limitations are transcended. Our mind develops limited concepts based on the appearances of what we receive through our limited senses. As soon as the conscious mind and imagination receive a natural picture through our sensory perceptual process, all the limitations of time, space, dimension, and motion are present in our conceptualization. In effect, these work like a cocoon surrounding our conscious mind, constraining and veiling what we "see." The conscious mind and the imagination also darken the intellect, creating an artificial image that we mistake for reality. These unreal halos cloak the essential attraction to knowledge, and do not allow true recognition, perception, and analysis by a metaphysical process. It is obvious that, through natural coordination of the senses, we "see" the body's cells, and although what we "see" is not complete, we craft laws that supposedly govern the cells based on time and space measurements. We must move beyond these constraints to the metaphysical realm of perception and logic to discover the mysteries of existence. Our senses work in their natural, systematic ways, but we can never open up the essence of nature by merely examining it externally.

Consider, for example, Kepler's and Newton's laws of planetary motion, laws which have been respected by the scientific community for centuries. Yet recently, the observation of a comet traveling at 550 kilometers per second at a distance of 5200 kilometers from the sun produced data which cannot be described by these same laws. Exceptional events clearly make the present laws fallible, reminding us that the truth is not yet known. Two further examples may be presented. Any object which has a specific weight on Earth is two and one half times heavier on Jupiter, yet much lighter on Saturn, and even lighter still on Pluto, a planet with a very small mass. These differences make us aware of relativity. Another instance is the scientific possibility of considering time as a fourth dimension within the limitations of a galaxy. This fourth dimension may appear to stand on its own conceptually, but when relativity is examined, the limited units and standards resulting from temporal comparisons seem illogical.

Cause and effect, motion and stillness, potentiality and deed are all affected by relativity, as in the examples above. Realistic comparisons are made and logic developed to explain every contradiction to our observations. Natural proportions change when they are analyzed individually or in different configurations. In that sense, any law or principle we examine must be reassessed; its validity is intrinsically woven into the initial set of assumptions. The names and definitions of a square, triangle, circle, or straight line are agreed upon by general consensus. But much of our world cannot be contained within general standards. For example, in the Earth's twenty-four hour rotation, every second has its own position and appearance, yet it follows gravitational laws with complete regularity. Another example is the apparent disorderly movement of gases. Although, to us, it appears irregular, the movement of gas still obeys specific natural patterns that are regular. The patterns are similar to what happens when we attempt to make a ball of a fifty meter piece of yarn: To do so, the point of intersection between our fingers has to be irregular. If we cross the yarn at the exact point repeatedly, we will not produce a round ball. Similarly, if we were to make a law for the motion of an electron's mobile point, we would need to use seemingly irregular motions, like those of gases. This is very similar to Sir James Hey's[17] hypothesis that the origin of the stars' orbital patterns is based on the instability of gases.

We currently do not have the capability to chart the course of an irregular particle from its inception to infinity. Therefore, we discard the irregularities of motion and proportion from our formulations. This prompts us to believe in regularity as a universal, general law, causing us to rely on it.

Our tendency to look for order is founded on the observation that nature generally exhibits inherent order. If creation had a beginning point and we could observe and track all motion of every atom and their organization, then we would see and understand the apparent irregularity of gases. The idea of an ultimate, all encompassing pattern is believable, and if we examine nature scientifically we begin to comprehend its truth.

When I look at a blossom, fresh and beautiful, I ask myself where it comes from. What is the source of its elegant, graceful, orderly beauty? How do its roots interlacing the soil find the essence of life and tenderly transmit these essentials through its branches and leaves? It is similar to observing a painter, mixing his colors on his palette, working carefully to create what he sees. He is detached from everything else and is governed by his inner vision, which he attempts to reproduce slowly and precisely. He ignores his surroundings and focuses on just one place. Slowly and precisely, he gives life to the delicacy of his mind and spirit. The flower follows its destiny, never stopping or making a mistake. As though drawn by a brush on the tableau of nature, it works slowly and precisely until a beautiful flower appears. We can ask in which part of the roots this delicate, beautiful, fragrant flower was hidden. How does it bloom? What atmospheric and magnetic waves and sun rays help this flower to grow? Who arranged this? What is it seeking? I can smell the fragrance that permeates the air around it. The flower acts like a beautiful baby, making everyone appreciate its elegance and grace. It seems to want to be everywhere for all time. Where does this eagerness to exist in eternity and infinity originate? Where and what is the secret and mysterious power that directs this flower? Our minds cannot truly recognize or perceive this power. If these natural effects and manifestations are examined with a scientific eye, we will assuredly shorten our passage to understanding. This understanding will, in time, open our way to the true and mysterious force that guides the flower to grow and allows it to reach for the sky.

The only thing that is obvious is that this perpetual, strong driving force, which works without diversion or interruption to reach its destination, is the mastermind of nature. The destiny of existence and the actions and reactions of its individual particles are evidence of this Divine Force.

All life forms, wild plants and animals, the dense forces of stones and minerals, even the selfish human being, are under the influence of the same force. Like the process of water evaporation, everything is being absorbed, moving toward heaven in the love attraction toward eternal destiny. Even our own suspended sphere in space, the planet Earth, circles in the sky, already in the heavens. What does this Earth, circling the sun, want, and where will it find what it is attracted to? Where would we search for this Divine Force, as we move through space, day and night, toward an unknown point?

Who or what is exerting this force that propels, guides, and directs the universe? Who is its commander, what is the plan, and where is He? Everything in existence is attracted to this powerful, precise, eternal commander in proportion to its capability. What does this nonstop attraction mean? How can He not be everywhere when His command is everywhere? Does He exist apart from existence, or does existence remain apart from Him? If one is not preoccupied and busy with others, one will begin to recognize one's own truth and the realities of existence.

Spinoza said that the mind and the body are not separate; they are two different manifestations of the essence that is God. Therefore, God is the body and the essence, the soul and the heart. God is able to influence everything because God is all at the same time, and in reality is Himself. There is no other essence than God.

یا مرتضی علی
کتبه الفقیر شاه مقصود

Sixth Manifesto

As a man's heart and conscience open
and his inner vision and consciousness expand,
the greater is his awakening
to the wisdom and knowledge of existence.
The acute awareness of his own ignorance
is every man's first solid step
toward a greater knowledge of existence.

Although his connection with nature appears unique, the wisest person is he whose personality is in harmony with the essence of nature and the truth of Existence.

Some small sample of everything in the universe can be seen in a person's being; this accounts for the human being's eminent status. What keeps people in disarray and unaware of their miraculous position however, is their dependence on their senses and the subsequent natural dispersion of their energy. If each person refined himself, and erased everything from his being but God, removing all images and dependencies, he would reach the state of omnipotence with which God has entrusted him. In their own truth, humans are the essence of nature, the essence of all Existence; this is the Kingdom of God.

Abol Abbas Almoli[18], one of the great Sufis of his time, was once asked to perform a miracle. He replied, "What greater miracle is there than my own life? I used to be a butcher, slaughtering sheep day after day and selling them to people. Once the spark of God's mercy opened my heart, I was led to saints like Abu Saeed Abel-Kheyr[19] to speak of His Blessing." The supreme knowledge Abol Abbas spoke of is not the kind of acquired learning gained through books and lectures. It is the harmony of inner knowing mentioned earlier. When he closed his eyes to all external attractions, the inner vision of his heart opened to his true self. He began to know meaning instead of appearance. Gradually, he eliminated everything superfluous from his being, until he found unity and oneness with the essence of Existence.

The way of the truly wise human being is both simple and difficult. The sensitivity of the enlightened mind possesses the feminine quality of exploring things keenly and deeply, noting every detail, without the feminine tendency of becoming absorbed by the surface of things. The quality of seeking the depth of meaning beyond external observations is also necessary. It seems that both masculine and feminine qualities have been combined by Existence and are displayed in their ultimate form in the truly wise.

The greatest of wise men throughout history are those who experience and exhibit both great tenderness and compassion for the weak and oppressed, and who also demonstrate supreme strength and courage in following the path of God's will. This balance and perfect completion allows them to be a benchmark for all humanity in distinguishing between appearance and truth. Their guidance serves humanity in the way a lighthouse guides ships away from harm.

I have seen many people who claim to be scholars and educators and who thoughtlessly spend their time analyzing how others came to know and understand Existence. They attempt to discover how the great thinkers' minds work and how great scientists made their discoveries. Their greatest accomplishment is to pass judgment on the works of others. This careless type of investigation leads them along a long, involved and fruitless path, for their real objective is lost. Their energy and time is wasted, no matter how grandly their work is presented.

I remember a time some years ago when I was invited to an educational and cultural seminar that a friend of mine was hosting. The speaker was unable to attend that night and my friend anxiously turned to me asking me to give the lecture. I gratefully and selfishly agreed, though I called it friendship and cooperation that day. My friend was pleased and appreciative and went on his way, smiling. I then gave an unprepared speech about a subject that I had not carefully researched or examined. The audience was as receptive as they would have been to any speaker, and I presented a melange of past and present ideas about science, psychology, and literature. My goal was to free my friend from his anxiety and worry, and to impress the audience with my knowledge and eloquence. My reason for relating this experience is to point out that it is a common occurrence among leaders and speakers. Often we see speakers presenting pretty images and using ideas in eloquent ways, with audiences responding positively. Yet no one knows or learns anything. The wise refrain from rambling speech and excesses over trifles; and they are cautious not to mislead or merely impress the audience.

It is not my intention to criticize anyone who attends meetings or speaks at gatherings. My hope is merely to convey that whenever we make a presentation, we must present what we truly know from our own experience. The purpose of informing the audience and not taking them for granted needs to be given serious consideration.

There is a mutual agreement that usually takes place when a speech is given. The speaker arouses the audience, and the audience, with a continuous nodding of heads, tends to confirm everything the speaker says. But what this mutual agreement means must be examined. It this a selfish exercise of mutual arousal, or is there something noteworthy being taught? The mind must be valued for its true significance. Enlightening the public, studying values, or explaining scientific discoveries should never be underestimated.

Hegel[20] said that there are always truths and mistakes, rights and wrongs, among people and their thoughts; yet searching, finding, and sharing truth is the job for a great man. A person who can discover, experience, and teach what is needed in his time is a truly great man. Therefore, if a man is well-known as a scholar and speaks eloquently, but is of no benefit or use to his audience, then he is merely selfish. Some years ago, I met a man who was very famous and renowned in his field. I was truly astonished when, the moment we met, he started talking and continued on and on without pausing to see if I had any interest or questions. He talked because he wanted to hear himself talk. His purpose was not to help me understand anything, but only to impress me with what he knew.

Saint Augustine[21] once said that truth remains hidden from man because he is so often the victim of what he needs to conquer.

Socrates, defending himself at his well-known trial, gave his own explanation. Chearephon went one day to the Temple of Delphi and asked Apollo, the sun god, if there was anyone wiser and more knowledgeable, than Socrates. A voice answered him that there was none more learned than Socrates. Socrates wanted to understand the meaning of this, for he knew that he was not very knowledgeable, but he also knew that God's words were true. So he took the time to truly examine himself. After a long period of reflection and consultation with other learned men, he came to this conclusion: God is the only one who is wise and knows everything. The wisest man knows his own ignorance, as did Socrates.

My master and teacher always said: "Superiority and virtue are found in listening ears and not in the speaking tongue." A wise teacher is in love with beauty and truth, and thus is a keen and receptive student, searching everywhere in nature to find what he loves. If a person doesn't praise himself with childish selfishness, but rather seeks to harmonize with truth, his capabilities will be greatly enhanced. Like the powerful crane that can lift many times its own weight, such a man is able to move the greatest mental and spiritual weight with a small expenditure of energy.

Herbert Spencer[22] has written that it is the understanding of the meaning of things that has value in any sort of mental, ethical, physical, or educational effort. Otherwise, one merely acquires words and language, while their true meaning is never mastered and events are never understood.

True knowledge comes through the soul's recognition and harmony with the truth of nature. Beyond sensory perceptions and emotional reactions, one can touch and experience nature, and all of existence becomes known. It is in this experience that one realizes one's limited knowledge and thus becomes intimately aware of and connected to infinite existence. It is in this way that the knowledge of the soul is perceived through nature, as man searches for the way from his internal world to infinity.

Kant[23] stated that beauty does not show us the state of the external world; instead, it shows us the beauty within our own soul. The beauty hidden within us recognizes the essential power of beauty and resonates with it. As with music, we relate from our inner soul as our potential is touched, like a tuning fork.

"He is the Ever Alive, the Eternal."

Seventh Manifesto

Death is an evolutionary and developmental
stage of being.
It is the tearing away of the veil
that covers the infinite absolute.
Death and life are two reciprocal appearances
that become thought of as stages of existence.
In reality, however, existence is an absolute whole
which contains these steps.

Birth and death are clear, natural, and precise images of change that follow an evolutionary pattern. Predestined, they move toward the freedom that has already been prepared in the universe. In the opinion of physical and metaphysical scientists, the foundations of birth and death extend through physiology and anatomy to psychology and ethics. The essential soul stimulates evolution in the world of possibilities and presents many appearances, harmonizing the conditions of its being.

Before entering life in this world, the soul has ascended through many levels of ability and capacity on the evolutionary ladder. Following the same principle, it follows and accepts the equipment of the body and the organization of physical life to continue its natural life. Thus, after death, it must neutralize the effects of the previous conditions, and move forward in the continuous journey, obtaining new equipment to harmonize with the environment. It follows this evolutionary pattern until it reaches a state of absolute freedom. It is this process that Descartes describes in his statement that every change in this world has a role in the totality of existence.

In his book *On the Principles of Nature*, Leibniz presents the concept that birth gives us ample time to study and investigate its process. Death, however, appears to reverse its process very suddenly, making it difficult to observe this progression. If there were a certain intensity in the changes from life to death, we would understand birth, death, and the traces of life in fossil remains, primitive animals, and the cylindrical bacteria and primitive algae which still exist today. The multiplication of green algae and the reproduction of some types of bacteria represent this process of evolution that has been carefully studied. Yet in our limited understanding of the journey of particles and energy throughout natural existence, the wondrous mystery remains. We do see again and again, however, the general principal that perfection comes gradually and works precisely as it leads nature in the desired direction. Perfection gradually and precisely guides nature through the transcending changes, although these gradual changes cannot all be seen by the careful eye of the researcher. What we can see is nevertheless astounding, as we witness that existence is always held in a delicate balance between life and death. One observable example of this gradual and immeasurable change is that of the yearly shedding of a snake. Although it is not precisely observable, the molting follows a prescribed order. Similarly, a pan of water on the stove heats up slowly until it starts to boil; the change takes place gradually, but in the eyes of an observer, it happens suddenly, with in a small amount of time. This same progression of endless sets of transformations happens everyday, everywhere in existence. There is nothing that arrives suddenly, out of nowhere, or disappears in an instant. Instead, there are endless comings and goings, births and deaths, although it may appear to us that these are sudden events.

Understanding and believing this relationship of a continuous, ongoing evolution may seem like severing the link between cause and effect. In reality, there is no cause without effect and nothing is possible without a constant, all-encompassing spiritual force. The effects that we see are like a newborn child, whose possibilities were developed in the mother's womb.

The soul has been studied extensively throughout human history in an effort to understand humanity. By definition, it may be said that the soul is free of any attributes, corruption, or embellishment. Sometimes the soul manifests itself as human knowledge or human nature, sometimes as the key to life, and sometimes it appears riddled with corruption. The soul reflects the eternal essence of man, and is limitless and free. Marcus Aurelius[24] has said that whatever comes from the soil will return to it, and whatever comes from the heavens will return to the heavens.

The confusion about man's essential nature persists. The problem is that the attachment of the secondary nature of our identity, which surrounds our essential being and the natural cycles of our existence, stays with us until our second birth. Buddha[25] said, "After my new birth, death ceases." These layered conditions are the instruments of human identity. Death appears to us as a finite event, a definite boundary, yet throughout nature continuity is an omnipotent pattern, though its forms and colors change.

If one distinguished any pattern in the phenomenon of natural existence regarding the truth of identity, he would understand the essence of life after death. These different states of being and non-being are like isthmuses with a common boundary. Although they seem to be separate intervals, they do not have distinct and separate boundaries. Like the spectrum of light described by Newton, the different colors can be differentiated by the observer. Each color has different specifications; red is distinguished from green and has different wavelengths. These wavelengths have all been measured from 1/1000 of an angstrom to 3000 microns. Yet in a natural reflection, as observed from a prism, there is no distinct boundary between these colors. Gradually, red becomes orange, yellow, amber, green, blue, violet, and ultraviolet. We can only approximately represent the spectrum. Although the colors have different appearances, there are no distinct boundaries between them. Similarly, isthmuses contrast life and death, even though life and death are born of each other. They are continuous states of existence. The unity and order which prevails throughout nature are aspects of the fundamental law of Existence. Continuity is invariably present in everything.

Thus, the materialistic view that matter dominates nature, especially regarding human existence, must be questioned. Hegel wrote that human beings are temporal states of eternal essence, evolution, and potential. But if we compare our temporary "life" with eternal time and space, we become aware of our nothingness, our existential condition.

Materialistic thought is based on hypothesis drawn from conclusions about natural, limited, observable changes. This view cannot and will not recognize the principal of existential originality through the developmental process and order of assimilated natural changes. In fact, the effective way of researching complex problems is not to merely accept what is observable and deny anything our senses cannot define. It is unjust to placate our minds with simplistic conclusions.

A discussion I had with a friend may help to illustrate these points. There are many good reasons to believe in the eternity of the soul, and no need to deny the eternity of matter or energy, or the principal that nothing is lost in the universe. My friend insisted on materialism as the explanation of the universe: namely, that the universe is nothing but a mechanistic, unconscious, unintelligent world. And he wanted to convince me of this. My mind being open to new ideas and knowledge, I do not blindly accept or reject methods or thoughts. But it is unwise to accept theories that do not have a strong foundation in observation, experiment, experience, and rational thought.

I endeavored to explain to my friend about the being of the human being, from his microscopic form to his changes through time. I described the continuous changes that are taking place throughout the body, from the molecular and cellular level up through the organizational processes of systems and organs. I explained how these systems and organizations of cells are eventually replaced by other phenomena after their forms change. Clearly, there is continual change in their appearance before birth, during lifetime and after death.

The cells of the brain and nervous system change very slowly, so people think they are eternal, or at least stable through a lifetime, recording and organizing memory. But the body cannot give a person a stable, consistent identity because it is continuously changing. Very simply, matter cannot be the cause of the body because it is always in flux. We continue to misunderstand this because identity is always contiguous with matter, and our limited senses perceive the bodies as organs that are part of our overall identity. Our confusion about this is also based on our belief that our sensory experiences are true knowledge, even though upon examination those too often prove unreliable. Our senses are the tools of our identity. So the question is how we can define ourselves by a standard that is constantly changing. And what is constant and unchanging? We continuously analyze matter, searching it for the stable essence, but it is not to be found there.

There is a hypothesis in physics that states that the inner energy of a body equals zero. Those who espouse materialism have sometimes used this hypothesis to demonstrate their position. They believe that the world is merely a composite of automatic, mechanistic actions and reactions. Since no real example of this exists, they use a clock to demonstrate their point.

In my earlier work, *Chanteh*, I explained how throughout nature it is clear that cause manifests effects. It confirms the creator and creation; in other words, creation simply attests to the creator. If we were to separate and analyze the initial thought of the inventor, which is his reality, from the instruments of the invention, no invention would remain because we would have separated it from its true principle.

Let us continue using the example of a clock. Before the invention of clocks, a thinker studied celestial patterns and learned to compute time. He then visualized his idea, the clock, in his mind. Next, he developed the idea using what tools and materials he had to craft a clock. Once he had made the instrument, the clock began to work. The important point is that the inventor's knowledge is the necessary condition for the clock to exist and do its work. His reality -- his knowledge, know-how, and ability -- is built into the clock. Thus, knowledge is more essential than its constructs. If, however, we try to separate knowledge from what it has constructed, the outcome has no meaning and makes no sense. The clock's existence results from the inventor's knowledge. The clock and its workings are the tools of the inventor, the traces of his being.

The inventor and his knowledge are necessary for every invention. The creator is the critical necessity for the created. The instruments and appliances of the invention are not essential to the inventor; it is the other way around. If a craftsman does not have the tools and equipment necessary to practice his trade, it does not mean he lacks the knowledge. These examples are a metaphor for the nature of the soul and its relationship to the body. The body is like the invention; it is the created corporeal manifestation of existence. The soul is analogous to the creator's knowledge. It exists and gives us life; it is there before our birth and after our death. This is the pure inner being, the absolute essence and eternal source.

My friend who believed in the philosophy of materialism had studied the ideas of John Stewart Mill[26]. Mill wrote that one's self-concept and character are a composite of memories based on sensory perception. He postulated that the mind stored past perceptions and attempted to calculate their possibilities in the future. This storing and comparing function thus gives the mind the illusion of a distinct self or identity that he calls "I." Conceptualizing external objects is also a product of the mind's process of associating sensory material that is imagined.

If we analyze these ideas we come to the following conclusions. Identity and personality are in constant change and have no constant point throughout a lifetime. Man's character is constantly changing and developing due to changeable, ongoing sensory perceptions; and because of this, the character of man is different from his past. Thus a newborn baby who has no developed sensory perception, has no identity. So who cries when the baby cries?

Consider a person with amnesia after an accident. Say he eventually regains his memory. During his period of memory loss, he functions normally but does not understand many things. Nevertheless, he tries to identify things and learn their use, much as a child would do. This striving to learn, to know, is an innate tendency, a manifestation of the inner essence or identity. This drive does not come from outside; it arises within the person. If his memory loss lasts for one year, during that time this individual accumulates sensory and natural experiences and examines them. Yet, at the end of that year, when his memory returns, he is like a person awakening from sleep. He takes up where he left off, discharging the year of experiences he struggled to understand. This raises many questions. Does he feel he has two identities? Do they know each other? Was there only one identity whose mental capabilities of memory were temporarily interrupted? The original identity demonstrates that its capability and knowledge have been maintained.

Throughout the body, all cells follow a set program separate from human will. They do not ask for help in order to live. They serve as a model, behaving according to the intrinsic knowledge of their essence. And they know what to do. Look at what happens when a virus enters the body. The body's systems act immediately and without our will or knowledge, for hours or days, until the body's temperature rises enough for us to notice there is something going on. Without the interference of human will, all of these actions continue until the risk of infection is eliminated and the corruption is destroyed. The physical cells work through various set processes with no spiritual or ethical qualities related to them.

Events and occurrences are not the organizers or developers of life's pattern. Instead, the original sources determine the boundaries and limitations of patterns by prescribing their intrinsic conditions. The qualities of human life are related to the electromagnetic fields that are the intervals between layers of the body, waves, and the soul. They determine boundaries, or stages, and densities according to their predestined dependence on nature. Their appearance within natural life is intrinsically determined within the nature of existence. Events and happenings are not the basis of this organization and development.

In any case, these continuous interactions and changes of waves and particles cannot produce a stable identity, or soul. When I look at my own life, I see many physical changes in my body. I see changes in my mind with things I have learned or forgotten. There was a time when my mind was blank and clear. Yet after all the years and all the experiences, I am still now as I was. Throughout all the changes, I still recognize myself; it was me doing whatever I did. It was "I" who initiated things, "I" who created things in my mind. All of the abilities of this "I" have come from eternal existence. This "I" is unlimited, and thus it cannot be described or defined by the limited expressions of the body. This "I" is stable and unchangeable at all times.

In his book, *The Way of Cognition*, Vivekananda[27] wrote that each person is comprised of a body, a self and a soul, or identity. This soul is hidden behind the self and the body. The self is the internal covering and the body is the external covering. The soul uses the body and self as its instruments, but, since it is not material, it is not subject to causality or change. It is eternal and undisturbed by emotion and external cycles. Because it is eternal, it has no beginning and no end.

So my true essence, which is unchanged throughout my lifetime, existed, I believe, before my birth, and will continue to exist after my death.

Krishna[28] has said that this world has been built by His hands, but He is not seen by everyone. Everything has its being through His power and potential. Everything is within Him, yet they are not His essence. Ask yourself, what is this mystery? My soul can create everything I choose, yet it is free of everything.

Eighth Manifesto

The natural desires of man
and his endless longings
are thick veils
that are placed, one after the other,
between the vision of man's heart
and the truth.
This is how man is deprived
of his innate treasure chest of tranquillity,
and why he blindly accepts the inauthentic for the real.

If dreams concurred with human destiny and became real as soon as they arose in our mind, how different the world would be, and how quickly pain would dissolve. I have known people who are so engrossed in their own fantasies that their faces beam with a dance of joy. Their awareness slumbers like a buried treasure while they enact their fantasy worlds. Yet, like it or not, dreams and fantasies have no stability, as they are not built on a firm foundation.

Immature and childish dreams and illusions fill the pages of our mind's book, and lead us to unreal conclusions decorated with colorful and beautiful patterns. They nurture hopelessness, misfortune, and coldness in our body and spirit. The deprived and needy develop dreams and fantasies of castles, gold, glitter, fine food and wine, romance, magnificent clothes, and magical encounters with famous people. They enjoy their fantasies and are stimulated by them either to be entertained or to lose themselves.

If these unrealistic dreams and fantasies, unfounded by anything but imagination, become strong and powerful and rule the heart and brain, we are led on a path of misfortune and disappointment. The face of these fanciful desires is not unlike the painted faces of prostitutes. Their appearance may be bright and attractive, but the pain of their self-betrayal has penetrated and damaged their very cells and turned them into dangerous, insensitive people. Those they seduce with their deceptive smiles must also bear the pain and misfortune that is given and taken.

Desires are endless and people are never satisfied, regardless of their situation. Possessions do not offer peace. Striving to fulfill desire is akin to irrigating an immense desert. No matter how much water is poured into it, the land remains dry and thirsty.

So who can find satisfaction pursuing his desires? Only a fool will ceaselessly try to find tranquillity in indulgence and disturbance. One who is so attracted to his fantasies chases a mirage created by a vain imagination. He can never enjoy the gift of the present and is forever anxious about the future. The person who consistently pursues his wishes spends himself chasing his own illusions. He is unaware of his true essence, and thus has lost the most precious treasure he will ever have. Sadly, he deprives himself of the assurance he so needs, and becomes hopelessly engulfed in despair.

Humans have always conceived of ways to free themselves from physical and spiritual misfortune. They have developed complex and simple programs, relied on them, and utilized them. In Buddhism it is said that if a person knows himself, he is not attracted or attached to earthly physical life. When there is true revelation, true understanding, our endless desires and longings naturally disappear. Ignorance is the path that fetters us to the world and its materials. Ignorance and knowledge are two opposite journeys in life. One who chooses knowledge will not be misled by the world's glitter or his body's urges. The path of ignorance leads only to endless wandering and empty striving. A person who knows himself is free; he is not swept away by joy or sadness. He is guided by his inner voice, and his concerns about past, present, and future needs do not overwhelm him.

Fichte[29] has said that the basis for ethical behavior and standards is knowledge. One who is ignorant cannot distinguish right from wrong and act accordingly. Each of us is always free; our actions reflect our inner state. We cannot enforce morality; it must come from within. Inner knowledge of goodness and the understanding to distinguish what is beneficial from what is harmful are the only constant, sure guideposts. Inner knowledge lights the right way like headlights on a dark road at night.

Research by scientists and geologists who have classified the age of fossils and minerals estimates that the Earth is over a billion years old. Some scientists believe that the Earth continues to evolve toward perfection in an endless journey. But many people are afraid to accept this truth, clinging instead to their traditional points of reference--family, culture, nation, etc. Their fear obstructs their view, and they believe that they will be dissolved into nothingness if they expand their perspective.

Throughout most of human history, people have felt helpless facing the forces of nature. The powerful forces of storms, earthquakes, darkness, oceans, and the sun are clearly so great that early humans assciated them with gods and began to worship them. They offered sacrifices and honored Jupiter and Mars, Neptune and Uranus, the sun and the moon. They prayed for protection from these 'gods', which they themselves created, begging for their favor. Hoping for safety and happiness, they often sacrificed all they had in the hope of future goodwill from these idols. In the event they received what they prayed for, they would credit their self created 'gods', not the power of their own belief that made their wish come true. These beliefs were supported by family and culture, and spread through societies with the repetition of stories and memories. Even today, we find examples of this kind of worship in some African tribes (the Bantu and Hottentot) and in other cultures of the world.

Early humans and primitive cultures had no knowledge of the forces of nature and feared their powerful effects. Out of ignorance they created idols that corresponded to the conditions of their time, and these idols were worshipped and venerated. These people would turn to their idols for help and protection. Naturally, with the passage of time, these beliefs were embellished and rituals were established. If these idols and 'gods' did not answer the needs and wishes of petitioners, other, more elaborate practices were developed. It is a person's individual belief, which can be called the God of Belief, that makes wishes come true. It is our own belief that accepts or rejects our prayers, yet throughout history humans has given this power to the idols that they themselves have created. What is credited to these idols is really the all-powerful miracle of belief.

This God of Belief, this spiritual antecedent to actual results, though deserving of understanding and gratitude, has largely been overlooked, while the concrete results of belief have been honored and cherished. As the gatekeeper of knowledge, belief is enormously strong and powerful.

Throughout all time, the deep strong call of awareness and truth has resonated behind the stories and masks that people continually create. Truth prevails in the midst of falsehoods, and the voice of belief continues to be heard. Within the primitive and the civilized, the pure and sensitive hear the call of truth in nature. Those who have the aptitude and capabiity to hear the call and follow it will be guided under any circumstance and at any time. It makes no difference what humankind does. If people worship an idol or a tree, or if they follow a spiritual path of guidance, truth is what it is, and it manifests itself. Wise and sensitive souls accept the path to actualization and serve as a guide for their time. The eternal truth, which Existence has given to human beings, has been so neglected in societies' activities and man's selfishness that it is hard for many to uncover it.

Xenophones[30] has said that if oxen and lions had hands and could paint like human beings, they would have undoubtedly painted their gods to look like themselves as humans have.

All of these common mistakes and misunderstandings, based on internal imbalance and instability, mislead and distract the youthful and the innocent. Instead of seeking self-knowledge, the most precious treasure we have, societies shortchange the young and teach them to yearn for illusive, imaginary goals. These goals or desires then become what is loved and worshipped, and the truth of life is completely overlooked.

Spinoza[31] wrote that the more a person knows his capabilities, the more he can effectively use his powers and abilities. Thus, the greater one's understanding of the wondrous order of the systems of nature, the more likely it is that one will avoid harm and the waste of unnecessary occurrences.

Thus, through this whole explanation, we can see that the generation and expansion of illusions and superstitions, reinforced through social tradition, misleads and misdirects sensitive and inquiring minds, as well as human potential.

Anyone who earnestly looks within himself finds some aspects of simple, universal, and essential truths. These truths can be the originator of one's intentions. Once a person starts to understand, his awareness grows. Instead of merely observing sensory input, one's potential can expand, develop, and shine like a beacon throughout one's lifse's journey.

Sadegh Angha

February 1954

ENDNOTES

[1]*RENE DESCARTES (1596-1650)*: French philosopher and mathematician. Sometimes called the father of modern philosophy. He was the originator of the Cartesian system of coordinates and curve plotting. In his book, *Discourse on Method*, published in 1637, he expresses his general skepticism as well as the reaffirmation of the strength and value of reason, saying about his own existence, "Cognito, ergo sum" - I think, therefore I am.

[2] *GOTTFRIED WILHELM LEIBNITZ (1646-1716)*: German philosopher and mathematician. He was an atomist and was the first to recognize the importance of the binary system of notation (systems or numbers based only on two states or symbols, 1 and 0) - a system crucial to the operation of modern computers. In 1671, he devised a calculating machine, and in 1684 he published important works on calculus. In 1693, he discovered the law of conservation of mechanical energy, subsequently generalized by others to include all forms of energy. He was an elected member of the Royal Society of London.

[3] *SIR ISAAC NEWTON (1642-1727)*: English scientist and mathematician. He is highly regarded as the discoverer of the theory of universal gravitation, the basic laws of motion, and the spectral theory of light. Apart from his superior achievements in many areas of physics, he was also the inventor of calculus, which he applied to formulate laws and solve problems. He was elected to the Royal Society of London in 1672. Like Democritus, Newton believed in the corpuscular nature of light, assuming that light consisted of a stream of particles moving in straight lines, which has certain elements in common with the modern quantum theory of light.

[4] *GALILEO GALILEI (1564-1642)*: Italian astronomer and physicist. Galileo was one of the first to herald the Renaissance of science and to stress the importance of quantitative experimental observations. His many contributions included the study of the motion of pendulums, falling bodies, projectiles, and telescopes, as well as the strength of materials. His discovery that objects of different masses actually fall at equal rate to the earth went against the contemporary belief due to Aristotle, but he experimentally proved the independence of the rate of fall from the object's mass by using inclined planes. His discoveries in mechanics were further developed mathematically by Descartes and Newton.

[5] *SHAMSEDDIN MOHAMMAD HAFEZ*: Fourteenth-century Persian Sufi poet. It is said that he was given the name "Hafez" as a title of respect for someone who has memorized the Holy Koran. Hafez mocked the hypocrisy of the clergy in his poems. His poems have been collected

under the title of the *Divan*, containing more than 500 poems, most of them in the form of *ghazals*, which are traditional and highly structured rhyming couplets. It was Hafez who inspired Goethe to compose his *West-östlicher Divan*. His poetry has been translated into many languages; its first English translation was completed in 1891.

[6] *HENRI BERGSON (1859-1941)*: French philosopher of evolution. He was professor of philosophy at the College de France, was elected to the French Academy and received the Nobel Prize in literature in 1927. Towards the end of his life, he was drawn toward religion and mysticism, believing that the mystic's spirit and love were humanity's only hope for a spiritual transformation.

[7] *SOCRATES (470 B.C. - 399 B.C.)*: Greek philosopher. Socrates is best known as an ardent lover of truth and knowledge and for his wit, humor, integrity, and courage. He used to lead arguments to compel his listeners and opponents to admit their own ignorance, even as he displayed modesty and pretended ignorance himself. The Oracle of Delphi proclaimed him the wisest of the Greeks (to which he said, "If I am the wisest, it is only because I alone know that I know nothing.") His strong views on following an ethical code of conduct and his sharp tongue caused him to be despised by many, however, and he was brought to trial in 399 B.C. on charges of atheism and treason. He faced the charges with courage and humor, and finally drank the poison sent for his execution.

[8] *PLATO (427 B.C. - 347 B.C.)*: Greek philosopher. Plato was a devoted follower of Socrates and became his disciple in 409 B.C. After leaving Athens following Socrates' execution in 399 B.C. and traveling for twelve years, he returned and founded a school that came to be known as the Academy, as it was on the lands of a prominent Greek called Academus (the name of this first university subsequently led to the use of the word 'academy' for educational institutes). He remained at the Academy for the rest of his life and died at the age of eighty. Plato's works include a series of dialogues presenting the discourses between Socrates and others, and focusing chiefly on moral philosophy. He was also very interested in mathematics (the Academy bore the inscription at its doorway, "Let no one ignorant of mathematics enter here."), and applied geometry to the description of the motion of the heavenly bodies.

[9] *COUNT MAURICE POLYDORE MARIE BERNARD MAETERLINK (1862-1949)*: Belgian dramatist and philosopher. Educated in law, he renounced the bar soon after his graduation and turned to writing poetry. He was interested in both mysticism and occultism. His hobby of beekeeping led to his search for mysticism and God in nature, and he studied and wrote on the lives of various insects. In 1911, he won the Nobel Prize for literature.

[10] *VINCENZO VIVIANI (1622-1703)*: Italian physicist. He was an assistant to Toricelli, and helped him in the invention of the first barometer.

[11] *EVANGELISTA TORRICELLI (1608-1647)*: Italian physicist and mathematician. Torricelli was a great admirer of Galileo and, in 1641, went to Florence to be Galileo's secretary and assistant. Upon Galileo's death three months later, Torricelli succeeded him as professor of mathematics at the Florentine Academy. Following a suggestion by Galileo, he became the first man to create a sustained vacuum and invented the barometer. However, he never published his barometer discoveries, as he was too involved in his studies of fluid projectile motion.

[12] *JOHAN KEPLER (1571-1630)*: German astronomer. Although trained to be a minister at the time of his graduation in 1591, Kepler developed interest in and taught science at the University of Graz in Austria. In 1597, he moved to Prague to work with the famed astronomer Tycho Brahe. In 1609, he published the results of the analyses of Tycho Brahe's accumulated observational data on planetary motion that eventually came to be known as Kepler's laws of planetary motion, and which proved to be a stepping stone for the formulation by Newton of the universal theory of gravitation. Kepler also wrote a story, the first work of science fiction, about a man who traveled to the moon in a dream.

[13] *CHARLES FRIEDRICH GAUSS (1777-1855)*: Gauss is regarded as one of the greatest mathematicians of all time. He was educated at the University of Götingen and made important contributions in the theory of curve-fitting, the construction of equilateral polygons, the theory of numbers, complex variables, and many other areas of mathematics. He was appointed director of the University of Götingen in 1807 and worked on terrestrial magnetism as well as several basic concepts of physics.

[14] *FRANZ ANTON MESMER (173401815)*: German physician. Mesmer, a mystic and astrologer, believed in the existence of cosmic forces affecting everything including human situations. In 1776 he obtained his medical degree at the University of Vienna and turned his attention to finding cures for diseases with the use of magnetic fields. Unfortunately, his successes in this venture were doubtful. He moved in 1778 to Paris, but a commission of experts set up to investigate his methods made an unfavorable report and he was forced to leave in 1785. He then retired and his technique subsequently came to be recognized by some as curing psychosomatic ailments by suggestion or hypnotism (also called mesmerism in his honor).

[15] *ÉVARISTE GALOIS (1811-1832)*: French mathematician. He is widely known for his 'group theory', which solved many questions in algebra that had previously seemed insoluble. He submitted three memoirs propounding his various mathematical theories and hypotheses to the Academy of Sciences in Paris, but all three were either rejected or lost. Shortly before he died in a duel, he wrote a last scientific testament which showed that he had been working on the beginnings of the theory of algebraic functions (which would not be fully developed until 40 years after his death).

16 *HERMAN LUDWIG FERDINAND VON HELMHOLZ (1821-1894)*: German physiologist and physicist. Helmholz studied medicine in Berlin, graduating in 1842 and practicing as a surgeon in the Prussian Army thereafter. He later taught anatomy and physics, invented the opthamolscope and contributed to the theory of three-color vision (now known as the Young-Helmholz theory), analyzed the scientific principles of the art of music, measured the speed of nerve impulses, and worked on non-Euclidean (Riemannian) geometry. His most important contribution, however, was his formulation of the theory of the conservation of energy, stating that energy is converted from one form into another (mechanical or kinetic, heat or thermal, light or electromagnetic, sound, potential, gravitational, chemical, etc.), but is never destroyed or created from nothing.

17 *JAMES STANLEY HEY (B. 1909)*: British astronomer. Hey did pioneering work in radio astronomy, the study of the sun, and predictions of meteorites.

18 *ABBOL ABBAS AMOLI*: Eleventh-century Persian Sufi. His insight and knowledge of the Holy Koran gave him unbounded facility in the sciences, and his eloquence, spiritual state and wealth of knowledge gained him the admiration of his contemporaries.

19 *ABU SAEED ABEL-KHEYR*: Eleventh-century Persian Sufi. He was one of the first to write his religious revelations in verse, in the 'rubai' form. Abu Saeed became acquainted with Sufism at an early age through his father's interest in Sufism. He completed his formal studies and then pursued his spiritual path, finally meeting Abu Abbas Amoli, through whom he gained his spiritual realization. His vast knowledge, facility in literature and his spirituality drew many devotees and admirers to his circle.

20 *GEORG WILHELM FRIEDRICH HEGEL (1770-1831)*: German philosopher. It is thought that Hegel's philosophy had an influence on many later philosophies, including existentialism and Marxism. After studying philosophy, Hegel became an admirer of Kant. In 1807, he wrote *The Phenomenology of the Mind*, which describes the development of the human mind from simple consciousness to absolute knowledge. Many disciples of Hegel hold that the key insight of his philosophy was that reality cannot be comprehended by analyzing different phenomena using separate categories of thought. Instead, according to Hegel, reality can only be understood as a comprehensive whole.

21 *SAINT AUGUSTINE OF HIPPO (354-430)*: Major theologian of the early Western Christian Church. After reading a work by Cicero, Augustine became interested in philosophy. He was particularly interested in Neoplatonism, which helped him to explain the nature of God and the origins of evil. Converted to Christianity in 386, he eventually became a proponent of religious predestination, which can be seen in his most famous book, *City of God*. Augustine served as the Bishop of Hippo in Roman Africa from 396 until his death.

[22] *HERBERT SPENCER (1820-1903)*: English sociologist. Spencer had little formal education and remained a lifelong bachelor. He started working in journalism in London around 1846, writing mostly on sociology and psychology. He believed in the evolutionary pattern of existence even before the publication of *The Origin of Species* by Charles Darwin, which popularized the terms 'evolution' and 'survival of the fittest.' Spencer advocated the practical application of these concepts in society, justifying brutal competition at the peril of the weak and advancing the doctrine of 'might is right.'

[23] *IMMANUEL KANT (1724-1804)*: German philosopher. Kant studied physics and mathematics, obtaining his doctoral degree in 1755, when he published *General History of Nature and Theory of the Universe*. However, he is best known as one of the greatest philosophers and as the author of *Critique of Pure Reason*, which was published in 1781. In the area of astronomy, he put forward the nebulae hypothesis about the formation of planets, and the suggestion that the Milky Way was a collection of stars and similar other galaxies ('island universes') existed. Under the patronage and protection of Frederick II of Prussia, Kant also contributed freely in the area of metaphysics.

[24] *MARCUS AURELIUS (121-180)*: Roman emperor and philosopher. He is famous for his spiritual reflections in his book, *Meditations*, which is considered a classic in Stoic literature.

[25] *BUDDHA (500 B.C. - 425 B.C.)*: Indian religious leader, originator of Buddhism. Born a prince, only son to the King of 'Kapilvastu' in Nepal near northeastern India, Sidhartha came to be known as 'Buddha,' or the enlightened one, after he renounced the royalty and all worldly attachments to wander the forests and meditate in search of the transcendental truth and, while in deep contemplation under a tree, one day attained it. He started preaching to a small group of disciples near Benaras in India, not far from the place of his enlightenment, and eventually a large part of Asia, including China, Japan, South-East Asia, Burma, Tibet, Sri Lanka, etc. came to accept Buddhism as a way of life.

[26] *JOHN STUART MILL (1806-1873)*: English philosopher and economist. Mill was a utilitarian and held the belief that every mind is a blank slate at birth. In his *System of Logic*, published in 1843, he developed his theory that mankind did not possess any innate morality, but that behavior was instead shaped by prior experiences. Mill also had strong opinions in economic matters. He was the first to add habit and custom to self-interest as economic motives, and, in his famous *Essay on Liberty*, advocated a minimum of governmental involvement in the lives of its citizens.

[27] *VIVEKANANDA (1863-1902)*: Indian spiritualist and philosopher. One of the greatest modern exponents and proponents of Indian spirituality, Swami Vivekananda assumed his name (Swami = a monk; Vivek = the inner power of discrimination between the real truth and illusory perceptions and untruths; Ananda = divine bliss and inner peace obtained through

enlightenment), in place of his given childhood name Narendranath Datta (Naren for short), after becoming the disciple of Shri Ramkrishna, a contemporary mystic-spiritualist in the tradition of the ancient sages. Shri Ramkrishna inspired Swami Vivekananda to become a monk, and later to come to the United States to attend the Parliament of Religions (Chicago, IL - September 27th, 1893).

28 *KRISHNA*: Hindu deity and mythological figure. Regarded as one of the incarnations or personalities of the supreme Godhead ('Vishnu'), Krishna is revered and worshipped in the Hindu tradition throughout India and across the world. Krishna is a central figure of one a popular epic, the *Mahabharat*, which was written by the sage Vyas. The exact time of composition of this monumental work is not known, but it is believed to be earlier than 5,000 B.C.

29 *JOHANN GOTTLIEB FICHTE (1762-1814)*: German philosopher and patriot. An admirer of Kant, Fichte wanted to establish a philosophy from which practical maxims to guide everyday life could be derived. He believed that man's inherent rationality would lead him to realize certain absolute moral laws, which it was man's duty to follow. Later in his life, Fichte's philosophy became more mystical and theological, and he began to realize that spirituality and faith could be far stronger than moral reason alone. By the end of his life, Fichte had written several treatises in which he spoke of the knowledge and love of God as the true end of life.

30 *XENOPHONES (570 B.C. - 480 B.C. approx.)*: Greek philosopher. Xenophanes was a contemporary of the mathematician Pythagoras, who is well known for his Pythagorean theorem on right angle triangles (the square of the hypotenuse equals the sum of the squares of the other two sides). Xenophanes postulated the emergence of the ground from the receding waters of the seas, based on the observation that sometimes sea shells are found on mountaintops. This is recognized as a valid assumption by modern geologists. Unlike many of his contemporaries, Xenophanes did not believe in the transmigration of the soul or in the multitude of Greek gods.

31 *BENEDICT DE SPINOZA (1632-1677)*: Dutch - Jewish philosopher. Spinoza was one of the leaders of the Seventeenth-century Rationalist movement. Due to his skeptical views, he was excommunicated by the synagogue in 1656. He admired Descartes' Cartesianism, but did not agree with its ideas regarding the transcendence of God and the distinction between mind and body. He used Descartes' geometrical method in his book *Ethica*, which presented metaphysics as a series of rational conclusions drawn from self-evident premises. He also advocated interpreting biblical sources historically, and not accepting all biblical stories as fact.

Genealogy of Maktab Tarighat Oveyssi Shahmaghsoudi
(School of Islamic Sufism)®

Prophet Mohammad
Imam Ali
1. Hazrat Oveys Gharani*
2. Hazrat Salman Farsi
3. Hazrat Habib-ibn Salim Ra'i
4. Hazrat Soltan Ebrahim Adham
5. Hazrat Abu Ali Shaqiq al-Balkhi
6. Hazrat Sheikh Abu Torab Nakhshabi
7. Hazrat Sheikh Abi Amr al-Istakhri
8. Hazrat Abu Ja'far Hazza
9. Hazrat Sheikh Kabir Abu Abdollah Mohammad-ibn Khafif Shirazi
10. Hazrat Sheikh Hossein Akkar
11. Hazrat Sheikh Morshed Abu-Isshaq Shahriar Kazerouni
12. Hazrat Khatib Abolfath Abdolkarim
13. Hazrat Ali-ibn Hassan Basri
14. Hazrat Serajeddin Abolfath Mahmoud-ibn Mahmoudi Sabouni Beyzavi
15. Hazrat Sheikh Abu Abdollah Rouzbehan Baghli Shirazi
16. Hazrat Sheikh Najmeddin Tamat-al Kobra Khivaghi
17. Hazrat Sheikh Ali Lala Ghaznavi
18. Hazrat Sheikh Ahmad Zaker Jowzeghani
19. Hazrat Noureddin Abdolrahman Esfarayeni
20. Hazrat Sheikh Alaoddowleh Semnani
21. Hazrat Mahmoud Mazdaghani
22. Hazrat Amir Seyyed Ali Hamedani
23. Hazrat Sheikh Ahmad Khatlani
24. Hazrat Seyyed Mohammad Abdollah Ghatifi al-Hasavi Nourbakhsh
25. Hazrat Shah Ghassem Feyzbakhsh
26. Hazrat Hossein Abarghoui Janbakhsh
27. Hazrat Darvish Malek Ali Joveyni
28. Hazrat Darvish Ali Sodeyri
29. Hazrat Darvish Kamaleddin Sodeyri
30. Hazrat Darvish Mohammad Mozaheb Karandehi (Pir Palandouz)
31. Hazrat Mir Mohammad Mo'men Sodeyri Sabzevari
32. Hazrat Mir Mohammad Taghi Shahi Mashhadi
33. Hazrat Mir Mozaffar Ali
34. Hazrat Mir Mohammad Ali
35. Hazrat Seyyed Shamseddin Mohammad
36. Hazrat Seyyed Abdolvahab Naini
37. Hazrat Haj Mohammad Hassan Kouzekanani
38. Hazrat Agha Abdolghader Jahromi
39. Hazrat Jalaleddin Ali Mir Abolfazl Angha
40. Hazrat Mir Ghotbeddin Mohammad Angha
41. Hazrat Molana Shah Maghsoud Sadegh Angha
42. Hazrat Salaheddin Ali Nader Shah Angha

*The conventional Arabic transliteration is Uways al-Qarani

PARTIAL LIST OF WORKS BY THE AUTHOR

Molana Shah Maghsoud Sadegh Angha, Pir Oveyssi
has written well over 150 books, treatises, essays and other works on *Erfan* in prose and verse conveyed through different disciplines. These include:

	Written	Published
Psalm of the Gods	1955	1963
Iron	1950	1950
Principles of Faghr & Sufism	1974	1987
The Sufi Miracle Commentary on the Holy Koran- 11 volumes	1962-1977*	
Owzan va Mizan (Weights and Balance)	1972	1973
Stages of Cognition in the Holy Koran	1972	1973
Manifestations of Thought	1950	1954
Message from the Soul	1960	1968
The Human Magnetic Body	1970	forthcoming
The Complete Arithmomancy	1967	forthcoming
Chanteh - Realm of the Aref	1940	1943
Life	1970	forthcoming
Microbic Sages	1951	1951
Two Pulse Beats	1973	forthcoming
Remembrance	1965	forthcoming
Al-Salat	1978	1978
Purification & Englightenment of Hearts	1978	1978
The Light of Salvation	1978	1978
The States of Enlightenment	1978	1978
The Hidden Angles of Life	1972	1974
Serr-ol Hajar	1960	1983
The Stages of the Seeker and the Ascent of Nader	1966	1983
The Mantle's Lineage	1945	1945
Through the Gates of the Unseen	1966	1983
The Traditional Medicine of Iran	1976	1978
Love and Fate	1938	1938
The Science of Numbers	1961	forthcoming
The Science of Names	1962	forthcoming
The Science of Coordinates and Squares	1962	forthcoming
The Principles of Oneness (The Epic of Existence)	1966	1968
Ghazaliat	1960	1984
The Star in Literature	1931	1932
Kymya	1961	1972
Golzar-e Omid (The Flowers of Hope)	1963	1964
Nader's Treasure	1940-1979*	
The Rightful Visions	1970	forthcoming
Psalms of Truth	1962	1964
Nirvan	1955	1960
The Heavenly Colors	1960	1984

*being compiled